Rain Forests

by Adele D. Richardson

Consultant:
Francesca Pozzi, Research Associate
Center for International Earth Science Information Network
Columbia University

Bridgestone Books
an imprint of Capstone Press
Mankato, Minnesota

Bridgestone Books are published by Capstone Press
151 Good Counsel Drive, P.O. Box 669, Mankato, Minnesota 56002
http://www.capstone-press.com

Library of Congress Cataloging-in-Publication Data
Richardson, Adele, 1966–
 Rain forests/by Adele D. Richardson.
 p. cm.—(The Bridgestone science library)
 Includes bibliographical references and index.
 ISBN 0-7368-0839-6
 1. Rain forests—Juvenile literature. [1. Rain forests. 2. Rain forest ecology. 3. Ecology.]
I. Title. II. Series.
QH86 .R53 2001
578.734—dc21   00-009807

Summary: Discusses the plants, animals, and climate of rain forest ecosystems.

Editorial Credits
Karen L. Daas, editor; Karen Risch, product planning editor; Linda Clavel, designer and
    illustrator; Heidi Schoof, photo researcher

Photo Credits
Erwin & Peggy Bauer/Tom Stack & Associates, 14
International Stock/Buddy Mays, 16
James P. Rowan, 1, 6
Mary Clay/ColePhoto, 20
PhotoDisc, 5, 7, 9, 11, 13, 15, 17, 19, 21
RubberBall Productions, cover
Unicorn Stock Photos/Marshall Prescott, 12; Dick Keen, 18
Visuals Unlimited/Ken Lucas, 10

1 2 3 4 5 6 06 05 04 03 02 01

Table of Contents

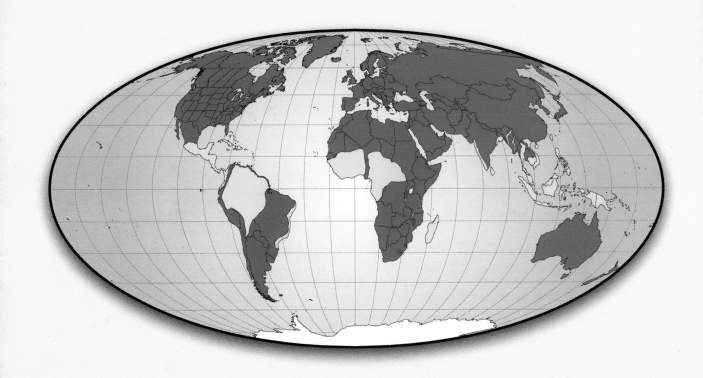

Rain Forest Facts

- Rain forests cover 6 percent of Earth's surface.
- Almost all rain forests are near the equator.
- The largest rain forest is the Amazon Rain Forest in South America.
- Between 60 and 400 inches (152 and 1,016 centimeters) of rain fall in rain forests each year.
- The average rain forest temperature is 68 to 93 degrees Fahrenheit (20 to 34 degrees Celsius).
- More than half of the world's different kinds of plants and animals live in rain forests. More than 30 million types of insects live there.
- People pick more than 50,000 tons (45,400 metric tons) of Brazil nuts from the Amazon Rain Forest each year.

Rain Forests

Most rain forests lie near the equator. This imaginary line circles the middle of Earth. The warm air near the equator helps rain forest plants grow. Some temperate rain forests also grow in North America and Australia.

Rain falls in rain forests nearly every day. Most rain forests receive more than 96 inches (244 centimeters) of rain each year. More than 360 inches (914 centimeters) of rain falls in some rain forests. This much water can flood areas of rain forests.

More types of trees and plants grow in rain forests than anywhere else on Earth. More than 250 different trees can grow in a 2-acre (1-hectare) area. Scientists have not explored some rain forests because the trees grow too close together.

The dark, leafy canopies of rain forests affect Earth's temperature. The dark colors of rain forest canopies absorb heat from the sun. These green roofs help keep the planet cool.

Millions of types of trees and plants grow in rain forests.

emergent layer

canopy

understory

forest floor

A rain forest has four layers. The top layer is the emergent layer. Only the tallest trees make up this layer. The treetops shoot above the rest of the forest's trees. Some emergent treetops reach more than 200 feet (60 meters) high.

The canopy layer lies under the emergent layer. Crowded tree branches form a green, leafy roof. The canopy is about 100 to 150 feet (30 to 45 meters) above the ground. Monkeys, birds, lizards, and insects live in the canopy.

The next layer is the understory. It is about 50 feet (15 meters) above the ground. Little sunlight reaches the understory because of the thick canopy. Snakes and insects live in the understory.

The bottom layer of a rain forest is the forest floor. The forest floor receives no sunlight. It is very dark and wet. Few plants grow on the forest floor. The dampness and darkness cause leaves and logs to rot quickly.

Tree leaves in the emergent and canopy layers keep sunlight from reaching the forest floor.

Animals in the Rain Forest

Many animals and insects live in rain forests. Some of these animals make their homes in trees. They move from branch to branch, never touching the ground.

Rain forest animals have adapted to the rain forest climate. Many rain forest animals use color for protection. Birds with green feathers blend in with tree leaves. Birds with bright yellow or white feathers often look like flowers in the trees. Poisonous insects and frogs are red, yellow, or blue. These colors warn enemies of danger. Other nonpoisonous animals sometimes copy these colors to trick their predators.

Monkeys, anteaters, and climbing porcupines live in rain forest trees. These animals have a prehensile tail that helps them move around. The tail can grab onto tree limbs and vines like an extra arm. Sloths also live in rain forests. They spend much of their time upside down in trees.

Two-toed sloths use their tail to help them move around.

Plants in the Rain Forest

Rain forest plants grow at many layers of the rain forest. Epiphytes are air plants that live in the canopies. These plants hang from tree branches. Their roots dangle in the air below. Ferns, mosses, and orchids are some types of epiphytes.

Lianas are woody, vinelike plants that climb up trees. Some lianas grow to be more than 3,500 feet (1,000 meters) tall. Lianas sometimes kill the trees they are climbing. They then start to climb another tree.

Bromeliads also grow on trees. The leaves of these large plants catch rain that falls from the tree. Insects and small animals make their homes on and near bromeliads. Birds flock to bright bromeliad flowers. They eat the insects that live there.

Hundreds of types of trees can grow within a small area of a rain forest. These trees provide shelter for rain forest plants and animals.

Bromeliads grow on tree trunks. Their bright flowers attract insects and small animals.

The Rain Forest Ecosystem

The trees, plants, and animals in a rain forest are part of an ecosystem. The climate also is part of the ecosystem.

Millions of plants and animals live in a rain forest. These plants and animals depend on each other. They form a food chain. The plants produce their own food using water and energy from the sun and soil. Smaller animals eat the plants. Larger animals then eat smaller animals. Animals rot and fertilize the soil after they die. They then become food for trees and plants.

Rain forest plants and animals also are affected by the warm and wet climate. Many plants and trees grow well in the rain forest climate. The trees shelter animals and plants. Animals drink water stored by plants.

Animals rely on trees and plants for shelter. Animals hide from predators in trees. The animals blend with the tree leaves or bark.

Parrots eat berries that grow on rain forest plants.

The Amazon Rain Forest

The Amazon Rain Forest is the largest rain forest in the world. It stretches across northern South America. The Amazon covers 2.5 million square miles (6.5 million square kilometers). This area is about nine times the size of the state of Texas.

The Amazon supports more types of plants and animals than anywhere else on Earth. Scientists have studied more than 1,000 types of mammals and lizards there. They think that the Amazon is home to about one-third of the world's birds. Scientists have not yet studied millions of plants and animals that live in the Amazon.

The Amazon River flows through the Amazon Rain Forest. This waterway is about 4,000 miles (6,400 kilometers) long. Many types of fish live in the Amazon River. Some catfish grow to be 10 feet (3 meters) long. Piranhas also live in the river. These meat-eating fish have sharp teeth. Piranhas will eat cows, or even people, if they fall into the river.

Trees and plants grow close together in parts of the Amazon Rain Forest.

Rain Forest Resources

People cut down rain forest trees for lumber. They build furniture, boats, and houses from the wood. They also make bowls and crates. People weave rope, baskets, and several types of cloth from tree fibers.

Much of the food people eat grows in rain forests. Workers pick bananas, coconuts, cashews, and peppers. Cola, which is in soft drinks, grows in rain forests. Spices such as cinnamon, ginger, and vanilla also grow there.

Several types of medicine are found in rain forests. Doctors treat high blood pressure and heart problems with medicine made from rain forest plants. Oils from rain forest trees are in cough drops.

People make many household products from rain forest trees and plants. They produce candles, sunscreen, and soaps. They also make perfume and chewing gum.

Cocoa trees grow in rain forests. People use cocoa to make chocolate.

Shrinking Rain Forests

The world's rain forests are shrinking. People sometimes take too many resources from rain forests. Many scientists believe the loss of rain forests will cause Earth's atmosphere to become hotter. Some people replace rain forests with crops. These lighter colored plants cannot absorb as much of the sun's heat.

The rain forests' trees absorb carbon dioxide from the air. Trees use this gas to make food. More carbon dioxide enters Earth's atmosphere when trees are cleared. The gas traps the sun's heat and may cause the planet to become hotter. Scientists call this temperature increase the greenhouse effect.

Animals in the rain forests suffer when people cut down rain forests. Animals lose their homes and food. As a result, many animals die.

Some people are trying to save rain forests. They harvest crops that benefit rain forests. They teach people about the value of rain forests.

People cut down rain forest trees to clear an area of land. They burn the remaining stems and soil.

Hands On: Watch Plants Drink

Plants and trees absorb water from the ground. Water travels through a plant's roots and leaves. You can see how water travels through a plant.

What You Need

Cup	An adult
Blue or purple food coloring	Knife
A stalk of celery with leaves	Ruler

What You Do

1. Fill the cup with water.
2. Add 15 drops of food coloring to the water.
3. Have an adult cut the celery about 3 inches (8 centimeters) below where the leaves start.
4. Place the celery in the colored water. Let it sit for two to three hours.

You will see colored streaks inside the celery. The streaks are the colored water that has been absorbed. Plants in the rain forest absorb water through their stems in the same way.

Words to Know

atmosphere (AT-muhss-fihr)—gases that surround a planet

canopy (KAN-uh-pee)—the layer of leaves and branches formed by the tops of the highest trees in the rain forest

carbon dioxide (KAR-buhn dye-OK-side)—a gas with no smell or color found naturally in the air

ecosystem (EE-koh-siss-tuhm)—a community of plants and animals interacting with their environment

emergent layer (i-MUR-juhnt LAY-ur)—the top layer of a rain forest made up of the tallest trees

prehensile (pree-HEN-suhl)—having the ability to grab onto things

understory (UHN-der-stor-ee)—the lowest layer of trees in a rain forest

Read More

Gray, Shirley W. *Rain Forests.* First Reports. Minneapolis: Compass Point Books, 2000.

Parker, Jane. *Rainforests.* Saving Our World. Brookfield, Conn.: Copper Beech Books, 1999.

Savage, Stephen. *Animals of the Rain Forest.* Animals by Habitat. Austin, Texas: Raintree Steck-Vaughn, 1997.

Useful Addresses

Canadian Organization for Tropical Education and Rain Forest Conservation
Box 335
Pickering, ON L1V 2R6
Canada

Rain Forest Action Network
221 Pine Street
San Francisco, CA 94104

Rain Forest Alliance
65 Bleecker Street
New York, NY 10012

Internet Sites

Amazon Interactive
http://www.eduweb.com/amazon.html
Rain Forest Action Network: Kids' Corner
http://www.ran.org/kids_action/index1.html
Zoom Rain Forest
http://www.enchantedlearning.com/subjects/rainforest

Index